Aim Your Child Like an Arrow

Vikki Burke

Aim Your Child Like an Arrow
ISBN 1-890026-01-8
© 1997 by Vikki Burke
P.O. Box 150043
Arlington, Texas 76015

Fifth printing June 2001
25,000 copies

Unless otherwise indicated, all Scripture quotations are taken from the *New American Standard* translation of the Bible.

Table of Contents

Chapter 1

Aim Your Child Like an Arrow

"Like arrows in the hand of a warrior, So are the children of one's youth."

Those 15 words in Psalm 127:4 paint one of the most powerful portraits of parenting illustrated in the Bible. They reveal the awesome privilege God has given parents, the privilege of fashioning their children into obedient, faithful and responsible adults. God's plan and desire is that our children be trained for success, and He's called us to do it. He's called us to prepare them like a skilled craftsman fashions an arrow.

You see, God created children to win. They were born to be successful by the working of God's Word in their hearts and lives. The Word works in their hearts when parents develop and nurture a hunger for God's Word in them. Only then can a parent truly aim them for the success God intended them to achieve.

Unfortunately, too many children have been conditioned to lose—maybe not intentionally, but they have been conditioned by a form of child abuse that gets little attention. They have become victims of neglect.

Several years ago the Duke of Windsor visited the United States, and when asked what impressed him most in this country, his much-publicized response was,

"The way American parents obey their children."

His comment was as tragic as it was humorous. But he described quite accurately the consequences of the neglect many children suffer.

If a parent doesn't aim a child, teach a child to hunger and thirst after God, then the child will seek outside influences to meet the need the parent should have met. It leaves the child to raise himself and miss the mark of all that God created him to be.

You've probably seen this kind of behavior. It's all around us. It is the root of much teenage delinquency, and it causes children who are not getting the attention they crave from their parents through normal means, to get it elsewhere. It is child abuse in one of its most devastating forms.

Aim Your Child for Success

Instead of being left to flounder and fail, constantly missing the mark of what they were created to be, God wants children to be taught His Word by parents who demonstrate it moment-by-moment in their lives:

> And these words, which I am commanding you today, shall be on your heart; and you shall teach them diligently to your sons and shall talk of them when you sit in your house and when you walk by the way and when you lie down and when you rise up (Deuteronomy 6:6-7).

How important is it that we take this command seriously? I have found the answer in the Bible account of two fathers who acted

8

quite differently. Lot (Abraham's nephew) and Noah (several generations before Lot) faced similar circumstances and challenges in raising their families in wicked and corrupt generations—much like we often feel today. Each of them had choices to make, choices that either made them strong in aiming their children or weak.

Failure in Responsibility

When put to the test, Lot failed in his choices—particularly two of them. His first mistake came when his uncle, Abraham, gave him the choice of where he wanted to live. Rather than choosing a godly place, he chose to settle near Sodom, a city known for its wickedness. The Scripture says it was *where the men were wicked and sinned against the Lord* (*see* Genesis 13:5-13).

Then, he developed a tolerance of sin and hesitated to obey God, a behavior that did not impress upon his family the importance of God's Word.

The Bible says this when the angels told Lot that the city of Sodom would be destroyed,

> And Lot went out and spoke to his sons-in-law, who were to marry his daughters, and said, "Up, get out of this place, for the Lord will destroy the city." But he appeared to his sons-in-law to be jesting (Genesis 19:14).

Lot's family did not respond to his direction—direction he had received from God. Why would they do such a thing?

Part of the answer is found in verses 15-16:

And when morning dawned, the angels urged Lot, saying, "Up, take your wife and your two daughters, who are here, lest you be swept away in the punishment of the city." But *he hesitated.* So the men seized his hand...and put him outside the city.

The failure of Lot's family to respond to his instruction should have come as no surprise. Lot himself was not quick to obey God's Word. His choices demonstrated to his children neither a hunger for God nor a respect for God's direction.

Because of these choices, his own family didn't take him seriously. Lot was more of a joke to his family than a man of integrity to be followed. Later as Lot and his wife left the city, Lot's wife disobeyed the command to "not look behind you" and was destroyed.

Lot was spared because of Abraham's covenant with God, but he lost his wife and other family members. And he received the greatest dishonor a parent could—his family mocked his instructions and did not respect his authority.

As a parent, Lot had failed in the responsibility God made so clear to Abraham,

> For I have chosen him, in order that he may command his children...to keep the way of the Lord by doing righteousness and justice... (Genesis 18:19).

The Secret of Noah's Success

Generations before Lot, however, another parent, Noah, faced similar challenges and succeeded:

> Noah was another who trust-
> ed God. When he heard
> God's warning about the
> future, Noah believed him
> even though there was then
> no sign of a flood, and wast-
> ing no time, he built the ark
> and saved his family. Noah's
> belief in God was in direct
> contrast to the sin and disbe-
> lief of the rest of the world—
> which refused to obey—and
> because of his faith he became
> one of those whom God has
> accepted (Hebrews 11:7, *The
> Living Bible*).

The example Noah set before his
family was that he "trusted God"
even though there was no physical
evidence to verify what he had
heard. His stand in faith—trusting
God for deliverance from the
coming destruction—gave his

children the opportunity to have his example as a pattern for their faith and to learn to trust him as their spiritual authority.

Notice that Noah "wasted no time" in obeying God. If he had hesitated like Lot, he would have jeopardized the lives of his entire family.

Noah's faith stood in direct contrast to the rest of the world "which refused to obey." Do you sometimes feel like you are the only one who believes God's Word, the only one with high standards for your children, surrounded by people whose beliefs are in direct contrast with yours? Well, you're not alone! Just continue to follow the Lord like Noah who determined to obey God regardless of what other people said or thought. Notice Genesis 6:8-9 says,

But Noah found favor in the eyes of the Lord...Noah was a righteous man, blameless in his time; Noah walked with God.

Notes in the *New American Standard* version translate the word blameless as "complete; perfect; or having integrity." Noah's life of integrity apparently had a significant effect on his children. Even though it had never before rained upon the earth, they followed him in building the ark.

What brought Noah this degree of respect from his children? The kind of respect that enables a parent to properly aim a child. He committed his life to responding to God's Word, and he faithfully trained his family to do the same. Because he lived uprightly in obedience to God, Noah's entire family was delivered from destruction.

He received the greatest honor a parent could—his family honored and respected him enough to follow his instructions.

Noah succeeded where Lot had failed—he lived a life of faith that held up God's Word as the standard. God's Word must always be the target to which you aim your child. Regardless of the skill of an archer, if he doesn't know where the target is, he will never hit it!

Set Your Sights on the Word

I call heaven and earth to witness against you today, that I have set before you life and death, the blessing and the curse. So choose life in order that you may live, you and your descendants, by loving the Lord your God, by obeying His voice, and by holding fast to Him; for this is your life and the length of your days... (Deuteronomy 30:19-20).

No one purposely lives under the curse. But many people find themselves there by default. Default means *failure to do something, or the absence of something needed.* Failure of a parent to love the Lord by obeying His voice will expose the family to the enemy's deceptions and attacks—even if the cause is ignorance or indecision.

Notice how important your decision is: "This is your life and the length of your days." Not even God can decide how you live. Only you can make that decision. The everyday choices you make and lead your children to make last the rest of their lives.

God's Word must always be your target. With practice, your children will learn it's not impossible to hit the mark. Hebrews 5:14 says that,

> ...solid food is for the mature, who because of practice, have their senses trained to discern good and evil.

Keep your children on target by developing in them a hunger for the solid food of the Word. Proverbs 22:6 tells us to, "Train up a child in the way he should go...." The Hebrew word *train* has its origin in a word which means *palate, roof of the mouth, taste.* This verse is referring to an ancient custom for weaning a child by developing his taste for solid food. According to custom, the mother would chew her food well, then put a dab of it on the palate of the child's mouth. Soon the child preferred the solid food to the milk.

In a similar way, you have been given the same responsibility regarding your child's hunger for God's Word.

So make the decision that you will take the time and effort to develop your child's palate to prefer God's ways. If you don't, their taste will be developed by others—others you probably don't approve.

For example, the television has become a modern day baby sitter that can cultivate attitudes of rebellion and defiance. The media is doing its best to shape the thoughts of young people to adopt liberal views of sex, homosexuality, drugs and violence. They are pressing to desensitize the minds of anyone willing to absorb their filth. Don't let the television raise your child.

And avoid letting your children spend the majority of their time with other children. This serves only to reinforce the foolishness bound in their hearts (Proverbs 22:15). "He who walks with wise men will be wise, But the companion of fools will suffer harm" (Proverbs 13:20). Your children need your help in uprooting foolishness and replacing it with wisdom. They need time with you, listening to you, receiving your counsel and advice on matters in their lives.

Keep Your Child on Target

Aiming your child like an arrow is a conscious, willful act. Look again at Deuteronomy 6:7,

> And you shall teach them diligently to your sons and

shall talk of them when you sit in your house and when you walk by the way and when you lie down and when you rise up.

Diligence. It's a decision backed by a commitment to hold fast to that decision. Making the firm commitment to teach your children "when you walk (or drive) by the way, when you lie down, when you rise up" simply means making the most of every conversation.

Just because you're a Christian and attend church faithfully does not guarantee your children are being taught your values. You cannot expect your children to get the direction they need from a couple of hours a week in church. The primary responsibility of aiming your children does not belong to the church. It belongs to you. Aim them at God's

Word, then be certain to check
them at regular intervals to be
certain they are still pointing in
the right direction.

Let everyday situations become
teaching times. Be open and
responsive to the Holy Spirit to use
these situations, not in a condemn-
ing way, but in an encouraging,
uplifting manner. God alone
knows the motivation of your
child's heart, and He alone can
reveal to you the most effective
way to reach him or her. As the
Scripture says,

Don't keep on scolding and
nagging your children, making them angry and resentful. Rather, bring them up
with the loving discipline
the Lord himself approves,
with suggestions and godly
advice (Ephesians 6:4, *The
Living Bible*).

Availability Creates Opportunity

Be certain your children are aware of your availability, no matter what you're doing. They should know they are most important to you, and you will stop anything to meet their need.

Make it a practice to talk about the Word in all your activities. When you take a walk or go to the park, use that time to develop an appreciation for God's creation, the birds, the beauty of the trees, the wild flowers, even the clouds in the sky.

Another opportunity for ministering the Word is bedtime. This is an especially powerful time to deposit into your children. They may have a special need for your comfort, love and approval, encouragement, assurance or just a listening ear. The words you speak before bed last all night and are there first thing in the morning.

Using a fun, casual atmosphere, you can be very effective in impressing powerful truths to your children. As a family, we frequently tell the stories about how God delivered us from Satan's grip; how He rescued us from a particular situation; even how God brought Dennis and me together to be married; and how God miraculously gave us a child when medically it was impossible. In this way, our daughter can grow to see God's Word as part of our everyday experience.

Shoot for Life, Not Just a Lifestyle

If your children are not to be drawn off target as they grow, they will need to see Christianity as not merely a lifestyle, but as *life itself!* Reach beyond the limitations of the mental realm and communicate with the heart of your children.

What have you trained your children to prefer? Have they developed a taste for the things of the world, or the things of God? Determine to model your life in such a way that it makes growing up something worth attaining.

Children learn by example. Impart wisdom to your children through your companionship. Cultivate and nurture friendship with them.

If you aim your child like the warrior would aim the weapon in his hand, you will not be ashamed. Your meaningful relationship with your children will cause them to see the truth and appreciate your wise counsel. And the joys of living in the promises of God's Word will bless them through eternity.

Chapter 2

God's Pattern for Parents

God has given every parent the privilege of molding children in a manner that will glorify Him. The generation we raise can live free from the bondages we had to overcome. With the Word of God that we have learned, we can teach even the youngest one to be victorious over the devil.

This privilege is also an awesome responsibility. God expects us to pattern our parenting after Him. He is a model worthy of imitation. Ephesians 3:14-15 says, "For this reason, I bow my knees before the Father, from whom

every family...derives its name."
Children form their image of God
from their parents. What image
of God are you portraying to
your children?

God does not father His children
through dictatorship, but through
relationship. God wants to have
fellowship with the man He
created. The Old Testament reveals
God's desire to dwell among His
people (see Exodus 25:8; 29:42-46).
But He wasn't satisfied with simply dwelling *among* them. So He
sent His own Spirit to dwell *in*
His people. His desire is to be
close, so close He lives within
every child of God.

In the same way, parents should
desire to have fellowship with the
child they have created. Such close
companionship means that the
parent truly delights in being with
the child. In Genesis 3:8, it says

that God walked in the garden looking for Adam and Eve. It was His practice to spend time with them as a friend.

God the Father placed man in a garden where all his needs were met. He is still willing to take full responsibility for the well-being of His children. He expects the same of us as parents.

Adam's purpose was to reflect the glory of God. Through man, God wanted to demonstrate His holiness, love, wisdom, comfort, faithfulness and grace. Man is to be the reflection of God's character.

God has given children an inborn desire to imitate their parents. Every child has said, "I want to be like my daddy or mommy when I grow up." Like a mirror, your children reflect your life. They will manifest the values you display.

The Importance of Time

Your child desires to be near you and to have fellowship with you. Children want their parent's company more than anything else that could be offered to them. It is rightly said, "Love is spelled T-I-M-E."

Children ranging in age from 5 to 18 were guests on a television program. The host asked each one this question: "If you could have anything in the world from your parents, what would it be?" From the youngest to the eldest, all answered essentially this way: "I would like to spend time with my parents." Your children, no matter how old, want a relationship with you! They crave it. They need it to feel right, to feel accepted and approved.

A relationship is a connection between two individuals. When a connection is made, there is a flow of power as with electricity. Some parents never make the connection that allows love to flow easily to and from their children. What a pitiful thought. You must come in contact with one another, and that doesn't mean simply being in the same room—it means flowing, joining and bonding together.

The modern idea that bonding occurs at birth when the mother first holds her child is shallow. Bonding is a process, beginning at birth, that lasts for the rest of your life! You and your children must be bonded in order to withstand the stresses of life.

A godly relationship binds and holds you together when things get tough. It's a uniting force, like a substance that cements parent and child, making both strong. The substance of bonding must be applied faithfully so it will adhere when it's needed.

In contrast, a parent who rules with absolute power is a dictator. The problem with dictatorship is that sooner or later it always causes rebellion. God did not make man to be controlled or oppressed! God made man to be free to choose the way he will live.

Your Choice Reveals Character

It is the grace of God toward all humanity that allows man to make this choice. Grace is defined in *Strong's Exhaustive Concordance* as, "God's divine influence upon the heart." God does not oppress His children; He influences them and draws them to Himself by the Holy Spirit. Romans 2:4 says it's the goodness or kindness of God that leads men to repentance, not harshness or control.

The right to choose is one of the greatest privileges you possess. Your true character is revealed as you express your will in free choice. Likewise, God's character is revealed through His will. His nature or character is to bless, heal, restore and give.

God's respect for your will is so great that He never forces a decision upon anyone. Deuteronomy 30:15 says, "See, I have set before you today life and prosperity, and death and adversity." The final choice is always yours.

God ordained the system whereby man could choose his lifestyle and receive the corresponding consequence. He clearly lays out the alternatives. If you choose life, the reward is prosperity; if you choose death, the penalty is adversity. The outcome is clear in advance, but the decision is up to the individual.

God designed man to have this freedom of choice. Shouldn't you, as a parent, equally respect your child's right to choose? You are to use every opportunity to influence the right choices, but you must guard his right to choose. Never force his choice; if you do, you are controlling him. The final responsibility of choice and its corresponding consequence is to remain with the child and not the parent.

Train Up a Child

It is the duty of the parent to train the child in right-doing. Throughout the child's training, he is to be presented very clearly with choice and consequence. Rules or boundaries should be clear and consistent. Without them, the child will be uncertain of what you expect and insecure about his actions and your reactions. Training lasts a long time, varying in focus with the child's age.

Your job is to influence your children. To influence means to, "produce an effect upon the actions or thoughts of; to persuade; to mold, to modify." Of course, this does not mean it's unnecessary to discipline your children with the rod; that is where "persuading" comes in.

To persuade is to induce or convince to a belief. When children choose not to be influenced and a rebellious act results, then they must be persuaded to make the right choice the next time! But that is a different subject entirely.

We *sway* a child to make a decision, or to go in a certain direction, *persuade* him to adopt a view or begin an action, and *mold* his character. Parents must sway their children to make the correct decisions in life with their influential training process.

You are to set before them the standard of the Word of God, which sways them. Often parents arouse their children emotionally, usually with threats, rather than inspiring them to keep the standard.

What is to be done when a child refuses to comply with a parent's request? His will is not changed by anger or force, but by gentle encouragement to a wiser, more excellent choice. Does it sound too easy? It is easy, when you conduct your household in this manner from the birth of the first child.

If your child refuses to cooperate, simply respond, "It is your choice to obey or disobey. You can do what I have asked or receive the penalty for your disobedience." This places the power in his hand and gives him a new desicion to make. Once again he is free to make a choice. If he continues in disobedience, he must receive the penalty—a spanking or whatever is appropriate. Now you are both released and can begin anew at the next decision.

In this manner, discipline and penalty are clearly linked to *his* choice and not to the issue or to the parent enforcing the penalty.

In contrast, if will-breaking is used to force a choice it will result in resentment, bitterness and rebellion. The thought that parents are to break the will of their child is totally against the character of God. Will-breaking has no part in the training of a child. A child with a broken will is not equipped to face the challenges of adulthood. Nor does a child with a broken will have the power to sustain the attacks of the world.

When talking about the will, I am referring to decision making or choosing between two possible actions. Training the will is to bring influence upon a child to choose or decide the right action. But to break the will is forcing action against one's choice, instead of influencing to choose the right direction.

Keeping With Their Individual Gift

Proverbs 22:6 in *The Amplified Bible* says,

Train up a child in the way he should go [and in keeping with his individual gift or

bent], and when he is old
he will not depart from it.

An important factor in training
your child is to acknowledge his
individual gift or bent. A gift is
a natural endowment, aptitude or
talent. A bent is a personal in-
clination, a strong liking, or favor
for something.

God has a unique plan and purpose for every child. It is the
responsibility of the parent first,
to seek God for that plan and
second, to keep with or follow
that plan.

But when parents impose their
own desires upon a child, it
becomes control. I have heard
parents say of a newborn, "My
son is going to be a prophet."
That's wonderful if God has
called him to that, but if He has
not, you are manipulating

instead of influencing. You cannot confess gifts and callings upon someone!

Realize that you must live a life of integrity before God, so your children will have a godly influence to pattern themselves after. This may require you to make some adjustments in your life, but that's good. One of the greatest functions of the Holy Spirit is His guidance. He will show you how to get on track and how to avoid snares and pitfalls. God's desire, as a Father, is that it be well with you (Jeremiah 7:23). He has plans for your welfare and not for calamity, to give you a future and a hope (Jeremiah 29:11).

Live a Life of Integrity

You must put the standard of God's Word before you and

determine to live by it! Deuteronomy 30:11 says,

> For this commandment which I command you today is not too difficult for you, nor is it out of reach.

God has not set anything before you that is too difficult for you to accomplish. God's will is within the reach of every believer!

If you continually make demands of your children that you are unwilling to fulfill yourself, they will rebel. I heard someone put it this way: "Rules without relationship create rebellion." The rules you make, you better keep!

The hypocritical words, "Do as I say, not as I do," never have produced good results because they are powerless. Second Corinthians 6:7

from the *J.B. Phillips Translation* says,
"Our sole defense, our only
weapon, is a life of integrity." If
you lack uprightness and honesty,
you have no defense or weapon.
But with a life of integrity before
God and His Word, you have
power that backs you.

The children of this generation
are crying out for something with
power, something that is real,
something that will put them
over. When you live according to
the Word of God, you have something they desire. Your children
will know that your life of
Christianity is not merely a public
display but the way you live
behind closed doors when no one
is looking.

Truly living by the standard
God sets before you as a believer
will cause your children to gravi-
tate toward you and toward the

Lord Jesus. People are drawn toward what is real and genuine. No one is attracted to a fake or a counterfeit.

The only way you can maintain a relationship with your children is to be genuine in your walk with the Lord. Children are experts at spotting a fake. My sister, Bonnie, told me that every time she thinks about her teenager she thinks, "REALationship."

When you are real, people respect you. You cannot demand respect, you must earn it. If your child lacks respect for you, he may obey on the outside, but on the inside he is rebelling. A life of integrity and uprightness before God brings respect.

The commandment to honor father and mother is given to children with the promise of a long life, full of blessing (Ephesians 6:2-3, *The Living Bible*). But if a child does not receive honor and respect in the home, he will not return it to the parent.

Remember Luke 6:38,

Give, and it will be given to you... For by your standard of measure it will be measured to you in return.

This scripture is not limited to money. If you were raised with honor and respect, you will give it to your children. If you were raised with criticism, you will give that unless you break its power and replace it with honor and respect.

It's not difficult to honor your child; merely regard him or esteem him as God's child. To honor your child does not mean that he rules

the house or has the right to inter-
rupt anytime or behaves without
proper discipline. To honor is to
give recognition, to treat with
respect and courtesy.

Children should be admired and
esteemed by their parents. Too
often they are looked on, not as the
blessing God said they are, but as a
burden and an annoyance.

God sees them with pleasure,
affection and approval. Remember that the manner in which
you view your children becomes
the way in which they view
themselves.

Stress-Free Parenting

Raising children doesn't have to
be filled with anxiety and stress, if
you follow God's ways and receive
His leadership and instruction for
your family.

When parenting God's way, day-to-day issues of parenting do not end up in constant fretfulness, anxiety and fear. Philippians 4:6 reminds us it is not God's will to be anxious and stressed out about *anything*, and that certainly includes raising children:

> Do not fret or have any anxiety about anything, but in every circumstance and in everything, by prayer and petition (definite requests), with thanksgiving, continue to make your wants known to God (*The Amplified Bible*).

Notice that God doesn't stop with just telling His people to not be fretful and anxious. He gives us the key to victory when the pressures, such as the normal pressures of parenting, do come: "...in everything, by prayer and petition (definite requests) make your wants known to God."

Praying for Your Children

Praying is one of the most important things you can do for your children. Children who don't have the support of their parent's prayers may struggle all their lives to know God and walk in His will. Even worse, they may never find it. But children whose lives are bathed in the daily prayers of their parents are on a path for a totally different outcome. A parent's prayers can be the very thing that empowers a child to make correct decisions. Daily petitions before God can make the difference in them being strong when peer pressure would otherwise persuade them to make the wrong decisions or follow the wrong crowd.

Vague, general prayers will

not bring this kind of success in parenting. As parents, we are to pray with purpose and power, presenting specific requests to God. God has given us His detailed handbook that contains the answers we need. Settle this beyond any shadow of a doubt: *You* have an audience with God. He cares about your needs. And He has the answers that are suitable both for your situation and for whatever your children are facing.

The Power of Praying God's Word

One of the most effective ways I have found to pray is to pray God's Word over my family.

Dennis and I were still babies in our walk of faith when we first discovered the power of praying God's Word. At that time in our marriage, I was a mess. I had a chip on my shoulder and was angry at everybody. Shyness tormented me. I could not speak to people and would never give my opinion on anything. I had never felt loved and didn't know how to love or how to receive love. Before I met Dennis, I had never experienced love. And even after marriage, I didn't trust Dennis. I lived in depression and isolation. What I had kept hidden from Dennis before our marriage became quickly and painfully obvious to him in our first few months together.

I was so worthless in my own sight that when Dennis would say things like, "I love you," I got mad at him and told him to shut up! I didn't believe him because I truly didn't believe anybody could love me. I thought all he was trying to do was make me vulnerable. I was resistant—resistant to him and resistant to God. I hadn't been raised with unconditional love, acceptance and confidence. The way I acted wasn't the way I wanted to be. It was just the only way I knew to be.

When Dennis discovered the enormous emotional baggage I was carrying, the only thing he knew to do was to tackle it by faith. Dennis could not approach me with the truth of what he wanted for me and what God had promised me without having me bark at him in resistance. So he began to speak to me while I was asleep. There beside me, night after night, he would softly speak the truths of who God had really made me to be in Christ:

"You are somebody."
"You're a person of worth."
"You're somebody worth loving."
"God loves you."

"You have an opinion and it's valuable."

"You have something to say to people that they need to hear."

He didn't know he was applying a biblical principle. He just felt in his heart he should do this. The only safe time he could do it was while I was asleep.

Those words of faith, spoken in the night, changed my life. Over the next year I began to experience revolutionary change. I began to share my thoughts and opinions and began to let my personality come forth. In a very real sense, for the first time in my life I became a person.

God's Words Will Transform Your Children

It was many years later that Dennis told me what he had

done. But following the prompting of the Holy Spirit, he was tapping into a principle we would later discover was echoed throughout the Bible. This principle is for anyone who will purposely speak words that agree with God's Word. The Holy Spirit will empower those words to come to pass.

The power God's Word can bring to any need is clearly revealed in Isaiah 55:10-11:

> For as the rain and snow come down from the heavens, and return not there again, but water the earth and make it bring forth and sprout, that it may give seed to the sower and bread to the eater, So shall My word be that goes forth out of My mouth: it shall not return to Me void [without

producing any effect, useless], but it shall accomplish that which I please and purpose, and it shall prosper in the thing for which I sent it (*The Amplified Bible*).

This scripture likens God's Word to the rain and snow that water the earth and produce fruit. When we speak the Words of God, they will not return to heaven and reach His ears before they have first accomplished His purpose. God has promised His Word will produce. His Words are filled with as much creative power today as they were the day He spoke them.

The Bible is full of promises that we can lay hold of and accept personally. Now, instead of praying vague, weak or ineffective prayers, we can take hold of the promises of God and pray them into existence. We can speak *His*

power-packed, creative words
into every area of our children's
lives and expect the results He has
promised. He promises His Word
will not be spoken without producing an effect. It will prosper in
the specific area it's applied to.
When we speak God's Word over
our children, it is like rain that
waters the earth and it will produce good fruit.

The important thing is that we be
not shaken if we don't *see* an immediate change. It may not look like
anything has changed in the natural realm. But when we speak His
Words, we are working in the spirit realm, and the natural realm
must come in line with the spirit
realm. As long as we won't faint
and give up but hold fast to our
confession, we will see the promise
of God fulfilled.

Remember, sometimes things

that have taken years to mess up take more than a month or two to correct! We have the promise of God from Jeremiah 1:12b that says, "For I am alert and active, watching over My word to perform it" (*The Amplified Bible*).

Believe God's Promises

When God spoke to Abram, he didn't allow unbelief or distrust to shake him or cause him to question concerning the promise of God. Even though his natural body was weak, he grew strong and was empowered by faith as he believed God's promise—regardless of how long it took!

You, too, can stand strong even in the face of seemingly hopeless situations. You can speak the Word of God, inserting your child's name in every verse that you pray. Anything you read can be yours by simply believing and receiving it. Speaking the promises of God's Word from your mouth confirms it as your own. What you are doing is using the same principle you used when you were born again:

That if you confess with your mouth Jesus as Lord, and believe in your heart that God raised Him from the dead, you shall be saved; for with the heart man believes, resulting in righteousness, and with the mouth he confesses, resulting in salvation (Romans 10:9-10).

The two steps that bring about salvation are (1) believing in the heart, and (2) confessing the Lord Jesus. This same scripture from *The Amplified Bible* says:

For with the heart a person believes (adheres to, trusts in, and relies on Christ) and so is justified (declared righteous, acceptable to God), and with the mouth he confesses (declares openly and speaks out freely his faith) *and* confirms [his] salvation (v. 10).

When you confess or declare something openly and speak your faith out freely, you actually confirm what you speak in your life.

Repeating a Prayer After God

You can better understand this principle by looking at the Greek word for *confess*—the word *homologeo*. This word was derived from two words which mean "to speak" and "the same." So it means "to speak the same." What your children need is for you to *speak the same* things over them and about them that God says. When you do, it's as though you are repeating a prayer after God.

The success God wants for you and for your children does not come by just knowing His promises. He wants you to appropriate them in every area of your life. God's plan is for you to live far above every circumstance of this world. He wants you to actively experience the reality and the power of His promises. But in order to see the manifestation of His promises you must say the same thing He says about your situation.

If this is new and sounds strange to you, remember what Proverbs 18:21 says about the power of your words, "Death and life are in the power of the tongue: and they that love it shall eat the fruit thereof" *(King James Version)*.

Say What God Says

Saying what God said was a principle John the Baptist used to answer those who questioned him about his ministry and who he was:

And this is the witness of John, when the Jews sent to him priests and Levites from Jerusalem to ask him, "Who are you?" And he confessed, and did not deny, and he confessed, "I am not the Christ." And they asked him, "What then? Are you Elijah?" And he said, "I am not." "Are you the Prophet?" And he answered, "No." They said then to him, "Who are you, so that we may give an answer to those who sent us? What do you say about yourself?" He said, "I am a voice of one crying in the wilderness, 'Make straight the way of the Lord,' as Isaiah the prophet said (John 1:19-23).

When John the Baptist was asked who he was, he did not just answer, but he *confessed*—he "said the same" thing God's Word had said about him. John purposely found the place in the Scripture that described him. Then he declared openly and spoke out freely what he believed about himself. He wasn't being arrogant, even though the religious people of his day may have thought he was. He was simply believing and receiving the promise of God for himself.

Jesus did the same thing at Nazareth:

And He came to Nazareth, where He had been brought up; and as was His custom, He entered the synagogue on the Sabbath, and stood up to read. And the book of the prophet Isaiah was handed to Him. And He opened the book, and found the place where it was written, "The Spirit of the Lord is upon Me, Because He anointed Me to preach the gospel to the poor. He has sent Me to proclaim release to the captives, And recovery of sight to the blind, To set free those who are downtrodden, To proclaim the favorable year of the Lord (Luke 4:16-19).

Notice Jesus purposely found the place where this scripture was written and read it, applying it to Himself. When He sat down He said, "Today this Scripture has been fulfilled in your hearing" (v. 21).

Praying the Promise

Over years of practicing just

what I have told you, I have com-
piled a notebook full of promises
that I have prayed for my daughter. The following scriptures are
some that I have used. I put my
daughter's name right in the
scripture to make it as personal as
I can. Insert the names of your
children in these scriptures and
begin today to pray God's Word
over them—no matter how old
they are!

More than anything, I want to
encourage you to pray and not
faint or give up if you don't
see immediate results. Let
Galatians 6:9 exhort you:

> And let us not lose heart and
> grow weary and faint in acting
> nobly and doing right, for in due
> time and at the appointed sea-
> son we shall reap, if we do not
> loosen and relax our courage and
> faint (*The Amplified Bible*).

The worst thing you can do is relax and loosen your faith on what God has said in His Word about your children simply because you aren't seeing results as quickly as you would like. You must refuse to be moved by what you see with your eyes because you have a promise! Don't forget that Jesus likened the Word of God to a seed that takes time to germinate and become fully mature:

> And He said, The kingdom of God is like a man who scatters seed upon the ground, And then continues sleeping and rising night and day while the seed sprouts and grows and increases—he knows not how. The earth produces [acting] by itself—first the blade, then the ear, then the full grain in the ear (Mark 4:26-28, *The Amplified Bible*).

God's Word is like a seed that takes nurturing to grow. Give it enough time to develop a root and sprout, then watch it flourish!

Through the promises of His Word, God is speaking to you, revealing His will and desire for your life. Believe them, and receive them. Receive His Word as a personal promise both for you and for your children. The promises are yours. Affirm them in your children.

Chapter 3

Daily Prayers

The following scriptures have been organized into topics that will help you locate them quickly. You can pray them all or only use the ones that apply to your situation. Of course, this list is by no means comprehensive. Add to it as you find something that applies to your situation.

Character

My children are the salt of the earth and the light of the world. They let their lights shine that the world may see their moral excellence and their good deeds and give honor to God (Matthew 5:13-16).

The grace of God trains my children to reject and renounce all ungodliness and worldly desires, to live discreet, temperate, self-controlled, upright lives in this present world (Titus 2:12).

My children love the Lord with all their hearts, therefore they do not love or cherish the world nor the things in the world. They are delivered from the lust of the flesh, the lust of the eyes, and the boastful pride of life (1 John 2:15,16).

All lust that ends in sorrow and vexation is removed from my children's hearts and minds (Ecclesiastes 11:10).

My children shun youthful lusts and flee from them. They aim at and pursue righteousness—all that is virtuous and good, right living, conforming to

the will of God in thought, word and deed. They are vessels for honor, sanctified and useful to the Master and prepared for every good work. They aim at and pursue faith, love and peace with others (2 Timothy 2:21-22).

God has given my children His great and precious promises so that through them they might escape from the moral decay and corruption that is in the world (2 Peter 1:4).

My children are not drawn to what is evil; they do not take part in or consent to the wicked deeds or the activities of those who are evil. They are kept and protected from the snares that are laid for them, from the traps set by evildoers. The wicked fall into their own nets, but my children escape and pass by in safety (Psalm 141:4, 9, 10).

My children keep their ways pure by keeping their lives in accordance with Your Word. They hide Your Word in their hearts so that they do not sin against You (Psalm 119:11).

My children do not make friends with people given to anger and will not learn the ways of an angry person nor become snared by them (Proverbs 22:24).

My children will not be deceived and misled by corrupt companions! Rather they fellowship with those of like precious faith, those with good morals, good character and manners (1 Corinthians 15:33).

My children do not speak polluted language, nor do they let unwholesome words come from their mouths. Instead, they only speak what is good and beneficial to others that it may be a blessing and give grace to those who hear. They do not grieve, sadden or offend the Holy Spirit (Ephesians 4:29-30).

The world will not squeeze my children into its mold. Instead, their hearts and minds are remolded by God's Word. They prove in practice that God, His will and His plans are good. They move toward the goal of true maturity (Romans 12:2).

Consecration to God and His Word

My children are disciples, taught of the Lord [and obedient to His will] and great is their peace and undisturbed composure (Isaiah 54:13).

My children hunger and thirst after righteousness. He pours His Spirit upon my offspring and His blessing upon my descendants (Isaiah 44:3).

The Lord pours His Spirit upon my children. My sons and daughters shall prophesy, and see visions and dream dreams (Joel 2:28).

My children hear, understand, and learn the Word of God; they reverently fear the Lord always and are careful to observe and do all the Word of God (Deuteronomy 31:12).

I diligently teach and impress my children with God's Word. They talk about the Word when they sit in the house, when they walk by the way, when they lie down and when they rise up (Deuteronomy 6:7).

My children put their trust, hope, faith and confidence in

God. They remember the works of God and keep His commandments. They are not stubborn or rebellious, but their hearts are loyal to God, and their spirits are steadfast and faithful to Him (Psalm 78:6-8).

Desires and Delights

My children delight themselves in the Lord, and He gives them the desires and secret petitions of their heart (Psalm 37:4).

My children earnestly desire and zealously cultivate the gifts and graces of God. They eagerly pursue and seek to acquire love and desire the spiritual endowments and gifts of God (1 Corinthians 12:31, 14:1).

My children delight to do God's will and will not forget His Word (Psalm 40:8, 119:16, 77, 92).

My children seek and inquire of the Lord daily and delight to know His ways, and He makes them to ride upon the high places of the earth (Isaiah 58:2, 14).

God, Who by the power that is at work within my children, is able to carry out His purpose and do super-abundantly, far over and above all that they dare ask or think (Ephesians 3:20).

The Lord hears the desires and longings of my children (Psalm 10:17).

My children live vitally united to God and His Words remain in them, so that they can ask whatever they desire and it shall be done for them (John 15:7).

The desires of my children shall be granted and bring only good because they are uncompromisingly righteous (Proverbs 10:24, 11:23).

I pray that God may grant my children their heart's desire and fulfill all their plans (Psalm 20:4).

God will pour out His Spirit upon my sons and daughters. They will see visions, dream heavenly dreams and prophesy (Acts 2:17-18).

The hopes of my children are not deferred, but their desires are fulfilled and become a tree of life (Proverbs 13:12).

I am confident that God has begun a good work in my children and will continue to develop, perfect and bring it to full completion (Philippians 1:6).

Favor

When my children found the Lord, they found life and favor (Proverbs 8:35, 12:2).

The favor of the Lord surrounds my children as a shield (Psalm 5:12).

The Lord is leaning toward my children with favor and regard for them, rendering them fruitful, multiplying them and establishing His covenant with them (Leviticus 26:9).

The Lord bestows beauty, delightfulness and favor upon my children. He confirms and establishes the work of their hands (Psalm 90:17).

My children continue to grow in favor with the Lord and with men and win the favor of everyone who sees them (1 Samuel 2:26, Esther 2:15).

By the favor of the Lord my children are exalted and walk with uplifted faces! (Psalm 89:17).

The Lord bestows grace, favor, honor and heavenly bliss upon my children. No good thing will He withhold from those who walk uprightly (Psalm 84:11).

Guidance

My children live and are controlled by the desires of the Spirit and set their minds on and seek those things which gratify the Holy Spirit, therefore they live in peace. My children are led by the Spirit of God (Romans 8:5, 14).

The Holy Spirit will guide my children into all truth for He doesn't speak of Himself, but He will tell them what He hears from the Father and will give the message to them (John 16:13).

My children hear and listen to the voice of the Good Shepherd.

They know Him and follow Him. He gives them eternal life, and they shall never lose it because no one is able to snatch them out of His hand (John 10:27-28).

The Lord guides my children continually and satisfies them in dry places. They shall be like a watered garden and like a spring of water that will not fail (Isaiah 58:11).

Health and Healing

Jesus bore grief, sickness, weakness, distress, sorrow, shame, and rejection for my children. He was wounded for their transgressions. He was bruised for their guilt and iniquities. The chastisement needful to obtain peace and well-being was upon Him. And with the stripes that wounded Him they are healed and made whole (Isaiah 53:4-6).

Jesus personally carried the sins of my children in His own body, so that they can be finished with sin and live a good life. For His wounds have healed them (1 Peter 2:24).

Christ has purchased freedom from the curse of the law for my children, having become a curse for them that they might receive the blessings of Abraham (Galatians 3:13).

The Lord heals my childrens' broken hearts and binds up their wounds, curing their pains and their sorrows (Psalm 147:3).

God sent His Word and healed my children and delivered them from destruction (Psalm 107:20).

My children attend to God's Word and incline their ear to His sayings. They do not let them

depart from their eyes, keeping them in the midst of their hearts for they are life and health to their flesh (Proverbs 4:20-22).

My children bless the Lord and do not forget the benefits of serving Him. He has forgiven all their iniquities, healed all their diseases, and redeemed their lives from destruction. He beautifies, dignifies, and crowns them with loving-kindness and tender mercy. He satisfies their mouths with good things, and their youth is renewed as the eagle (Psalm 103:2-5).

My children live in health and prosperity even as their souls prosper (1 John 2).

Honoring and Obeying Parents

Thank you Father for turning the hearts of my children and

reconciling them toward their parents. They are not disobedient or disrespectful. Instead, they give their attention to the wisdom of the righteous (Malachi 4:6 and Luke 1:17).

My children are obedient to their parents in all things, therefore they are well-pleasing to the Lord. I will not provoke or irritate or be hard on my children so that they will not become discouraged, inferior, frustrated or embittered against me in any way (Colossians 3:20, 21).

My children obey their parents in the Lord. Because they honor and esteem us as precious, everything is well with them, and they live a long life on earth. We do not irritate or provoke them to anger nor exasperate them to resentment, but they are brought up in the tender discipline, training and instruction of the Lord. They give us honor (Ephesians 6:1-4).

Knowledge and Wisdom of God

My children lean on, trust in, and are confident in the Lord with all their heart and mind and do not rely on their own insight or understanding. In all their ways, they know, recognize and acknowledge Him, and He directs and makes straight and plain their paths (Proverbs 3:5-6).

The Lord gives my children wisdom. He holds victory in store for them. He is a shield to them. He guards their course and protects their way. My children understand and do what is right, just and fair. They follow every good path. Wisdom enters their hearts and knowledge is pleasant to their souls. Discretion will protect them and understanding will guard them. Wisdom will save them from the ways of the wicked, from words that are perverse, and from those who leave the straight paths to walk in dark ways (Proverbs 2:6-15).

The anointing of God abides in my children. His anointing teaches them concerning everything (1 John 2:27).

The Holy Spirit teaches my children in the very hour and moment what they ought to say (Luke 12:12).

My children eagerly study and do their utmost to present themselves to God approved, having no cause to be ashamed, skillfully handling the Word of God. Their knowledge of the Scriptures makes them wise for salvation (2 Timothy 2:15).

Jesus Christ has been made wisdom for my children. All hidden things are revealed to them (1 Corinthians 1:30).

My children's memory is blessed because they have the mind of Christ. The Holy Spirit teaches them and will cause them to recall and remember all things that they need (Proverbs 10:17, 1 Corinthians 2:16, John 14:26).

My children have wisdom and knowledge and skill in all learning (Daniel 1:4).

God grants my children a Spirit of wisdom and revelation—of insight into mysteries and secrets—in the deep and intimate knowledge of Him. The eyes of their hearts are flooded with light so that they can know and understand the hope to which they are called and to know how

rich their inheritance is in Christ
(Ephesians 1:17).

My children increase in wisdom,
in full understanding, becoming
strong in spirit with grace, favor
and the blessing of God upon them
(Luke 1:80, 2:40, 52).

My children hear and receive
wisdom and the years of their life
shall be many. Because they walk
in skillful and godly wisdom,
their steps shall not be hampered,
and when they run, they shall not
stumble. My children regard and
attend to the wisdom of God as
life. They do not let His Word
depart from their sight but keep
it in the center of their heart.
God's Word is life and health and
healing to my children. They
guard their hearts with diligence,
knowing that's where the life of
God flows forth (Proverbs 4).

God has not given my children a spirit of fear, timidity or cowardice—but of power, love and a calm and well-balanced mind with discipline and self-control (2 Timothy 1:7).

My children are filled with the full knowledge of God's will in all spiritual wisdom, with insight into the ways and purpose of God and in understanding and discernment of all spiritual things. They are fully pleasing to the Lord, desiring to please Him in all things, bearing fruit in every good work and steadily growing and increasing in the knowledge of God with deep, clear insight (Colossians 1:9-11).

Overcoming Life

My children belong to God, therefore they defeat and overcome the spirit of the world because greater is He Who lives in them than he who is in the world (1 John 4:4).

In all things, my children are more than conquerors and gain a surpassing victory through Christ (Romans 8:37).

My children have strength for all things in Christ Who empowers them. They are ready for anything and equal to anything through Him Who infuses inner strength into them. They are sufficient in Christ's sufficiency (Philippians 4:13).

My children draw their strength from the Lord. They are clothed in the armor of God that they may successfully stand up against and resist the strategies and deceits of the devil (Ephesians 6:11).

My children are strong and

courageous. They shall not be afraid nor dismayed for the Lord is with them wherever they go. No man shall be able to stand against them all the days of their lives because the Lord God is with them and will not fail or forsake them (Joshua 1:5, 9).

My children overcome by the blood of the Lamb and by the words of their testimony (Revelation 12:11).

My children have confidence and assurance in God that when they ask anything according to His will, He listens to and hears them. And because they know He listens to what they ask, they know they have been granted their requests (1 John 5:14-15).

My children receive power and ability when the Holy Spirit comes upon them and wherever they go they will be His witnesses (Acts 1:8).

Protection and Safety

Because my children dwell in the secret place of the Most High they shall remain stable and fixed under the shadow of the Almighty [Whose power no foe can withstand]. He is their refuge and fortress, and on Him they lean, rely and confidently trust (Psalm 91:1-2).

For God will deliver them from the snare of the trapper and the deadly pestilence. He will cover them with His wings and they shall trust and find refuge; His truth and faithfulness are a shield and a buckler. My children will not be afraid of the terror of the night, nor of the arrow that flies by day, nor of the pestilence that stalks in darkness, nor of destruction (Psalm 91:3-6).

A thousand may fall at their side, and ten thousand at their right hand, but it shall not come near my children. They will only be spectators, inaccessible in the secret place of the Most High, as they witness the reward of the wicked (Psalm 91:7, 8).

Because they make the Lord their dwelling place, evil shall not befall them, nor any plague or calamity come near them. For God gives His angels charge over my children to accompany and defend and preserve them in all their ways. The angels shall bear my children up on their hands, lest they dash their foot against a stone (Psalm 91:7-13).

Because my children set their love upon God, He will deliver them. When they call upon Him, He answers them and is with them in trouble and shows them His salvation (Psalm 91:14-16).

Although the path to destruction is spacious and broad, my children walk on the narrow path which leads them to life (Matthew 7:13).

My children listen to wisdom and therefore dwell securely and in confident trust and shall be quiet, without fear or dread of evil (Proverbs 1:33).

My children can lie down in peace and sleep, for God alone makes them to dwell in safety (Psalm 4:8).

The Lord sends His angels before my children to keep them in the way and to bring them into the place that He has prepared for them (Exodus 23:20).

The Lord will keep my children from all evil; He will keep their lives (Psalm 121:7).

My children are not afraid, for the Lord will fight for them and they shall hold their peace (Exodus 14:14).

No weapon that is formed against my children shall prosper, and every tongue that rises against them in judgment shall be shown to be in the wrong. This peace, righteousness, security and triumph over opposition is the heritage of the servants of the Lord (Isaiah 54:17).

God guards my children, so that the wicked shall be silenced and the strength of men will not prevail (1 Samuel 2:9).

My children have nothing to fear for God is with them. He will strengthen them for difficulties. He will uphold them. All those who are enraged against them shall be put to shame and confounded, and those who strive against them shall be as nothing and shall perish (Isaiah 41:10-11).

The Lord is a rock, a fortress and a deliverer for my children. They put their trust in Him. He is their shield and high tower and refuge, Who saves them from violence. My children call upon the Lord and shall be saved from their enemies (2 Samuel 22:2-4).

The Lord is a refuge and shield for my children, who put their hope in His Word. God sustains them according to His promise, and they will live. He will not let their hopes be dashed. He will uphold them and deliver them (Psalm 119:114-116).

The Lord is shepherd of my children. He makes them to lie down in green pastures, He leads them beside quiet waters, He restores their soul. He guides them in paths of righteousness. Though they may walk through the valley of the shadow of death, they will fear no evil, for God is with them. His rod and staff comfort them. The Lord prepares a table before my children in the presence of their enemies. He anoints their head with oil; their cup overflows. Surely goodness and mercy shall follow them all the days of their lives, and they will dwell in the house of the Lord forever (Psalm 23:1-6).

Prosperous and Blessed

The offspring of my body is blessed of the Lord, and He makes them to abound in prosperity (Deuteronomy 28:4, 11).

Christ has redeemed my children from the curse of the law because He was made a curse for them that the blessing of Abraham would come upon them (Galatians 3:13).

My children diligently listen to and obey the voice of the Lord, therefore all the blessings of Abraham shall come upon them and overtake them. They are blessed in the city and the country. They are blessed in the fruit of their bodies and the fruit of their ground. They are blessed when they go in and when they go out (Deuteronomy 28:1-3, 6).

The Lord shall cause the enemies who rise up against my children to be defeated before their face. They may come against them one way and flee before them seven ways. The Lord commands the blessing upon their storehouse and in all they undertake (Deuteronomy 28:7,8).

All the people of the earth shall see that they are called by the name of the Lord and will be afraid of them. The Lord will cause my children to have a surplus of prosperity. He will open up His good treasury. My children shall be the head and not the tail, above and not beneath (Deuteronomy 28:10-13).

I fear the Lord and delight greatly in His commandments, therefore my children become mighty on the earth; and because I live upright before God they are blessed (Psalm 112:1-2).

My children are blessed, happy, fortunate, prosperous and enviable because they do not follow the counsel of the ungodly, (following their advice, their plans and purposes) nor stand in the path where sinners walk, nor sit where the scornful and the mockers gather. But their delight and desire is in the law of the Lord. On His law they meditate. Therefore, they shall be like a tree firmly planted by the streams of water, ready to bring forth its fruit in season. Their leaf shall not fade or wither, and everything they do shall prosper and come to maturity (Psalm 1:1-3).

As my children meditate on God's Word, they observe and do according to all they see. Then they will make their way prosperous and deal wisely and have good success (Joshua 1:8).

Because I have been made the righteousness of God and walk in

integrity my children are blessed
(Proverbs 20:7).

The Lord Jesus Christ has blessed
my children with all spiritual
blessings in the heavenly realm
(Ephesians 1:3).

God supplies all my children's
need according to His riches
in glory by Christ Jesus
(Philippians 4:19).

Salvation and Forgiveness

Because I have believed in the
Lord Jesus Christ [and have given
myself up to Him, taken myself
out of my own keeping and
entrusted myself into His keeping]
I am saved along with my household. My children receive Jesus as
their personal Savior and Lord
(Acts 16:31).

There is no God like my God,

Who forgives my children's iniquities and passes over their transgressions because they are the remnant of His heritage. He delights in mercy and lovingkindness (Micah 7:18).

Through the blood of Jesus Christ my children have redemption, deliverance and salvation, the forgiveness of offenses, shortcoming and trespasses (Ephesians 1:7).

When my children confess their sins, God is faithful and just, true to His own nature and promises, and will forgive their sins and cleanse them from all unrighteousness—everything not in conformity to His will in purpose, thought and action (1 John 1:9).

Christ has purchased freedom for my children and redeemed them from the curse and its condemnation by becoming a curse for them that the blessings promised to Abraham might come upon them (Galatians 3:13-14).

The accusing voice no longer nags my children because they are united to Jesus Christ. Their lives are directed by the Spirit rather than by old attitudes and patterns (Romans 8:1).

God forgives all my children's iniquities and heals all their diseases. He has removed their transgressions as far as the east is from the west (Psalm 103:3, 12).

The Lord blots out and cancels all the transgressions of my children and will remember them no more (Isaiah 43:25).

My children have been crucified with Christ. It is no longer they that live, but Christ the Messiah lives in them. And the life they now live, they live by faith, adhering and relying on the Son of God, Who loved them and gave Himself for them (Galatians 2:20).

My children live and walk in the Light. They have true fellowship and the blood of Jesus Christ cleanses them from all sin and guilt. They are saved and delivered by God's grace, being made partakers of Christ's salvation through faith (1 John 1:7, Ephesians 2:8).

My children have great peace because they love God's Word, and nothing shall offend them or make them stumble (Psalm 119:165).

My children do not hold grudges or become bitter and resentful. Instead, they are quick to forgive others so that their Heavenly Father will forgive them of all their trespasses (Matthew 6:14).

My children have become new creatures in Christ. The old previous moral and spiritual condition has passed away, and all things are fresh and new. Christ was made to be sin for my children's sake that they might become the righteousness of God, approved and acceptable in right relationship with Him by His goodness (2 Corinthians 5:17, 21).

Training, Discipline and Obedience

I am faithful and diligent to train my children in the way they should go, keeping with each individual bent or personality. When they are old they will not depart from it (Proverbs 22:6).

I will not punish my children because its result is guilt. Instead, I will train and discipline them with God's Word, which is profitable for instruction, for reproof and conviction of sin, for correction of error and discipline in obedience, and for training in righteousness. I do this so that they might be complete and proficient, well-fitted and thoroughly equipped for every good work (2 Timothy 3:16).

As a faithful, God-fearing parent, I do not withhold correction from my children. As a result, their souls are delivered from destruction (Proverbs 23:13-14).

I correct my children according to the scriptures, and they give comfort and delight to my soul (Proverbs 29:17).

The rod of discipline, administered in love and self-control, removes foolishness far from the hearts of my children. Foolishness is far from my children (Proverbs 22:15).

My children are wise, therefore they accept my instruction, correction and discipline. They do not have a mocking, scoffing spirit, but listen and heed my rebuke (Proverbs 13:1).

My children listen attentively to me and do not despise me. They do not reject or forget my teaching (Proverbs 23:22, Proverbs 1:8).

My children do not reject discipline but are wise, prudent and regard reproof. They make me glad (Proverbs 15:5, 20).

References

New American Standard Bible. The Lockman Foundation 1960, 1962, 1963, 1968, 1971, 1972, 1973, 1975, 1977.

The Amplified Bible (AMP). 1954, 1958 by the Lockman Foundation, La Habra, California.

The Living Bible (TLB). 1971 by Tyndale House Publishers, Wheaton, Illinois.

The New Testament in Modern English. J.B. Phillips 1958 by the MacMillan Company, New York.

Vikki Burke is the wife and ministry partner of Dennis Burke. Together they have affected thousands of people through a refreshing approach to God's Word. Their travels have taken them throughout the United States, as well as Australia, Asia, New Zealand, Canada, and the United Kingdom.

Dennis and Vikki began in ministry as youth pastors in Southern California where they obtained tremendous insight into the work of the local church. In 1976, they moved to Fort Worth, Texas, to work with Kenneth Copeland Ministries.

Compelled by the desire to see change in others, Vikki has delivered answers and insight to God's people. She has spoken at women's conferences, retreats and marriage seminars. She has brought encouragement to many in the body of Christ through the uncompromised Word of God.

People of Promise
Are Impacting Lives!

Every day someone is being changed by the power of God's Word through Dennis Burke Ministries. Reports come into our office daily about how God's Word has brought healing, hope, restoration to a marriage or salvation to a loved one. The Word of God is producing fruit for His Kingdom!

Our Partners are a vital part of all the work we are doing. Every person who is changed through this ministry will have our Partners to thank. A Partner is someone who joins with this ministry through their monthly financial giving and praying to help fulfill the Great Commission.

When you join in Partnership the anointing, favor and grace that rests on this ministry will rest upon you. When you have a need in your family, your business, your finances or whatever it might be, you can draw upon the anointing that operates in this ministry to help.

Also, as a Partner you will never be without prayer! Dennis, Vikki along with the staff pray for you. When you send your prayer requests we join our faith with yours for the anointing of God to remove every burden and destroy every yoke!

Even though our calling is to the world, our hearts are devoted to our Partners. That's why we designed a Collector's Series exclusively for our Partners—*People of Promise*.

The Collector's Series gives our Partners the opportunity each month to receive an exclusive teaching tape in which we have added a personal prayer and greeting.

When you send your first offering of $20.00 or more you will receive a beautiful Collector's Series album and the first tape in the series. Each time you send your monthly offering you can receive the next tape in the series by checking the box on your return envelope.

Join the *People of Promise* family by becoming a monthly Partner today. Fill out the coupon on the following page and send your first Partnership offering. We will join our faith with yours for God's best to be multiplied to you!

I want to join Dennis and Vikki in fulfilling the Great Commission. Enclosed is my first offering to become a monthly Partner.

$100 $50 $20 $15 Other $_____

Please send my Collector's Series album and my first Partner tape.

Name _____

Address _____

City _____

State _____ Zip _____

Phone (_____) _____

I sow this seed in faith believing that God will meet my need:

_____
_____

(B10)

BOOKS BY
VIKKI BURKE

Transforming a Distorted Self-Image
($2.00 – B18)

Stress Relief
($2.00 – B11)

The Power of Peace
($2.00 –B14)

AUDIO TAPES

Too Blessed to Be Stressed
($5.00 – DBM63)

**Pressing Through the Promise
Into Possession**
($15.00 – DBM50)

Burn With Passion
($10.00 – DBM56)

Relief and Refreshing
($10.00 - DBM49)

VIDEO TAPES

God Likes Things Hot
($15.00 - V114)

A complete catalog of books, audio and video
cassettes is available by writing:

Dennis Burke Ministries
P.O. Box 150043
Arlington, TX 76015
(817) 277-9627

*Please include your prayer requests
when you write.*

Visit our website at
www.dennisburkministries.org or
e-mail us at *Dbmin@aol.com*